# IRELAND

## A CELEBRATION
## IN VERSE

# IRELAND

## A CELEBRATION

## IN VERSE

*edited by*

ROY BENJAMIN

BARNES
&NOBLE
BOOKS
NEW YORK

1997 Barnes & Noble Books

ISBN 0-7607-0315-9

Book design by Jimmy Sarfati, Rocket Design

Printed and bound in the United States of America

98 99 00 M 9 8 7 6 5 4 3

QF

# Contents

# Introduction

❧

The Irish poetic tradition is an interrupted one. With its native Gaelic* displaced by English, the modern poets of Ireland have had to balance the claims of two traditions. William Butler Yeats affirms a connection to the English poets when he says, "Gaelic is my national tongue, but it is not my mother tongue," while Thomas Kinsella, with more grief and less assurance, simply recognizes that "I stand on one side of a great rift, and can feel the discontinuity in myself."

One way of bridging this gap is through translation. The great translators of the last century (above all Douglas Hyde and Samuel Ferguson) played a major role in the Irish Renaissance, which still exercises such an important influence on modern literature. The fact that there are today poets, such as Nuala Ní Dhomhnaill, writing in Irish owes something to their efforts. In fact, a third of the poems included here are translated from the Irish, and some—in particular "The County of Mayo" and "Cashel of Munster"—have been especially admired for capturing the rhythms of their Gaelic originals.

Though this collection is in some ways a record of historical

*The Celtic language whose variants are spoken in Ireland, Scotland, and the Isle of Man

grievance—English colonialism remains the defining catastrophe of Irish history—its purpose is not to glamorize nationalistic fervor but to show how grief has been transformed. Yeats is the great agent of transformation, in both Irish and modern poetry. It is interesting to compare "Easter, 1916" with the more didactic requiems of Thomas Osborne Davis and Charles Wolfe. What we have here is not a call to arms but a metamorphosis of the historical into the mythical. Similarly, Seamus Heaney's "Requiem for the Croppies" transforms the disaster of Vinegar Hill into a myth of resurrection.

This tendency appears in other sections as well. The literal exile mourned in "The Flight of the Earls" and "The Wild Geese" is treated figuratively in James Clarence Mangan's "Siberia," which Yeats calls "a sort of type of that Siberia within." Similarly, the historic downfall deplored by Padraic Pearse (executed after taking part in the Easter Rebellion of 1916) and Ferguson (who ends his poem with the exhortation to "Unite, oh, unite!") becomes in the work of John Montague, Seamus Heaney, and Medbh McGuckian the rendering of a divided consciousness. The Irish predicament becomes a symbol for the modern: the hope that an original dream language will survive a grafted tongue.

Yet the figurative can also be an evasion. Poems that celebrate the fabulous can be an escape from the real, and Yeats in particular, with his love of the mythical and mystical, has been criticized for not reflecting social realities in his poetry. In this light, Paul Muldoon's "Armageddon, Armageddon" can be read as a commentary on "Sailing to Byzantium," expressing the deflations that follow seasons of immortality. In the same way, J. M. Synge's "The Passing of the Shee" undercuts Yeats's "The Hosting of the Sidhe" with its desire to escape from the human.

But poetry does not uphold any single view of reality. The anarchic themes of love, humor, and intoxication are a needed refuge from the impositions of history: in this volume they balance out the more sobering themes of displacement, exile, and requiem. The curse also is a valued safety valve for the pressures of resentment. The word that can wound and kill is wielded more ironically by moderns like Synge and James Stephens, but still harkens back to an earlier time when words of power were part of the equipment of the Irish bard.

Above all, Irish poetry is diverse. The final section is meant to show something of the range of emotion Ireland itself has inspired, from Thomas Moore's idealizations to John Hewitt's bitter ironies, and to celebrate—as the poem ''Windharp'' does—the varying sounds of Ireland which coexist and intermingle ''till / the valley gleams.''

Roy Benjamin<br>1997

# places

A strong sense of place is one of the notable qualities of Irish verse. Few traditions display such a rooted love of the local.

# The Fair Hills of Ireland

A plenteous place is Ireland for hospitable cheer,
  *Uileacán dubh O!*\*
Where the wholesome fruit is bursting from the yellow
    barley ear;
      *Uileacán dubh O!*
There is honey in the trees where her misty vales expand,
And her forest paths in summer are by falling waters
    fanned;
There is dew at high noontide there, and springs i' the
    yellow sand,
On the fair hills of holy Ireland.

Curled he is and ringleted, and plaited to the knee,
      *Uileacán dubh O!*
Each captain who comes sailing across the Irish sea;
      *Uileacán dubh O!*
And I will make my journey, if life and health but stand
Unto that pleasant country, that fresh and fragrant strand,
And leave your boasted braveries, your wealth and high
    command,
For the fair hills of holy Ireland.

\*O dark lamentation!

Large and profitable are the stacks upon the ground,
     *Uileacán dubh O!*
The butter and the cream do wonderously abound,
     *Uileacán dubh O!*
The cresses on the water and the sorrels are at hand,
And the cuckoo's calling daily his note of music bland
And the bold thrush sings so bravely his song i' the forests
    grand,
On the fair hills of holy Ireland.

Translated by Samuel Ferguson

# *from* Prince Alfrid's Itinerary

I found in Munster, unfettered of any,
Kings and queens, and poets a many—
Poets well skilled and music and measure,
Prosperous doings, mirth and pleasure.

I found in Connaught the just, redundance
Of riches, milk in lavish abundance;
Hospitality, vigour, fame,
In Cruachan's land of heroic name.

I found in Ulster, from hill to glen,
Hardy warriors, resolute men;
Beauty that bloomed when youth was gone,
And strength transmitted from sire to son.

I found in Leinster the smooth and sleek,
From Dublin to Slewmargy's peak;
Flourishing pastures, valour, health,
Long-living worthies, commerce, wealth.

Translated by James Clarence Mangan

# The Little Waves of Breffny

The grand road from the mountain goes shining to the sea,
And there is traffic in it and many a horse and cart,
But the little roads of Cloonagh are dearer far to me,
And the little roads of Cloonagh go rambling through my
      heart.

A great storm from the ocean goes shouting o'er the hill,
And there is glory in it and terror on the wind,
But the haunted air of twilight is very strange and still,
And the little winds of twilight are dearer to my mind.

The great waves of the Atlantic sweep storming on their
      way,
Shining green and silver with the hidden herring shoal,
But the Little Waves of Breffny have drenched my heart in
      spray,
And the Little Waves of Breffny go stumbling through my
      soul.

Eva Gore-Booth

# The Lake Isle of Innisfree

I will arise and go now, and go to Innisfree,
And a small cabin build there, of clay and wattles made:
Nine bean-rows will I have there, a hive for the honeybee,
And live alone in the bee-loud glade.

And I shall have some peace there, for peace comes
    dropping slow,
Dropping from the veils of the morning to where the
    cricket sings;
There midnight's all a glimmer, and noon a purple glow,
And evening full of the linnet's wings.

I will arise and go now, for always night and day
I hear lake water lapping with low sounds by the shore;
While I stand on the roadway, or on the pavements gray,
I hear it in the deep heart's core.

William Butler Yeats

# The Meeting of the Waters

There is not in the wide world a valley so sweet
As that vale in whose bosom the bright waters meet;
Oh! the last rays of feeling and life must depart,
Ere the bloom of that valley shall fade from my heart.

Yet it *was* not that Nature had shed o'er the scene
Her purest of crystal and brightest of green;
'Twas *not* her soft magic of streamlet or hill,
Oh! no,—it was something more exquisite still.

'Twas that friends, the belov'd of my bosom, were near,
Who made every dear scene of enchantment more dear,
And who felt how the best charms of nature improve,
When we see them reflected from looks that we love.

Sweet vale of Avoca! how calm could I rest
In thy bosom of shade, with the friends I love best,
Where the storms that we feel in this cold world should
    cease
And our hearts, like thy waters, be mingled in peace.

Thomas Moore

# *from* Gougane Barra

There is a green island in lone Gougane Barra,
Whence Allua of songs rushes forth like an arrow;
In deep Valley Desmond a thousand wild fountains
Come down to that lake, from their home in the mountains.
There grows the wild ash; and a time-stricken willow
Looks chidingly down on the mirth of the billow,
As, like some gay child that sad monitor scorning,
It lightly laughs back to the laugh of the morning.

And its zone of dark hills—oh! to see them all bright'ning,
When the tempest flings out its red banner of lightning,
And the waters come down, 'mid the thunder's deep rattle,
Like clans from their hills at the voice of the battle;
And brightly the fire-crested billows are gleaming,
And wildly from Malloc the eagles are screaming:
Oh, where is the dwelling, in valley or highland,
So meet for the bard as this lone little island?

How oft, when the summer sun rested on Clara,
And lit the blue headland of sullen Ivera,
Have I sought thee, sweet spot, from my home by the ocean,
And trod all thy wilds with a minstrel's devotion,

And thought on the bards who, oft gathering together,
In the cleft of thy rocks, and the depth of thy heather,
Dwelt far from the Saxon's dark bondage and slaughter,
As they raised their last song by the rush of thy water!

Jeremiah Joseph Callanan

# Shancoduff

My black hills have never seen the sun rising,
Eternally they look north towards Armagh.
Lot's wife would not be salt if she had been
Incurious as my black hills that are happy
When dawn whitens Glassdrummond chapel.

My hills hoard the bright shillings of March
While the sun searches in every pocket.
They are my Alps and I have climbed the Matterhorn
With a sheaf of hay for three perishing calves
In the field under the Big Forth of Rocksavage.

The sleety winds fondle the rushy beards of Shancoduff
While the cattle-drovers sheltering in the Featherna Bush
Look up and say: ''Who owns them hungry hills
That the water-hen and snipe must have forsaken?
A poet? Then by heavens he must be poor.''
I hear and is my heart not badly shaken?

Patrick Kavanagh

# Displacement

$T$he decisive event in Irish history was the English invasion in the 12th century. Poem after poem returns to this catastrophe to deplore a common loss, remember a past greatness—and retrieve a lost language.

# Tara* Is Grass

The world hath conquered, the wind hath scattered like
 dust
Alexander, Cæsar, and all that shared their sway:
Tara is grass, and behold how Troy lieth low—
And even the English, perchance their hour will come!

Translated by Padraic Pearse

*Ancient seat of the high kings of Ireland

# from The Downfall of the Gael

My heart is in woe,
And my soul deep in trouble,—
For the mighty are low,
And abased are the noble:

The Sons of the Gael
Are in exile and mourning,
Worn, weary, and pale
As spent pilgrims returning;...

The Gael cannot tell,
In the uprooted wildwood
And the red ridgy dell,
The old nurse of his childhood:

The nurse of his youth
Is in doubt as she views him,
If the wan wretch, in truth,
Be the child of her bosom.

We starve by the board,
And we thirst amid wassail—
For the guest is the lord,
And the host is the vassal!

Through the woods let us roam,
Through the wastes wild and barren;
We are strangers at home!
We are exiles in Erin!

And Erin's a bark
O'er the wide waters driven!
And the tempest howls dark,
And her side planks are riven!

And in billows of might
Swell the Saxon before her,—
Unite, oh, unite!
Or the billows burst o'er her!

**Translated by Samuel Ferguson**

# John O'Dwyer of the Glen

Blithe the bright dawn found me,
Rest with strength had crown'd me,
Sweet the birds sang around me
Sport was their toil.

The horn its clang was keeping,
Forth the fox was creeping,
Round each dame stood weeping,
O'er the prowler's spoil.

Hark! the foe is calling,
Fast the woods are falling,
Scenes and sights appalling
Mark the wasted soil.

War and confiscation
Curse the fallen nation;
Gloom and desolation
Shade the lost land o'er,

Chill the winds are blowing,
Death aloft is going,
Peace or hope seems growing
For our race no more.

Hark! the foe is calling,
Fast the woods are falling,
Scenes and sights appalling
Throng the blood-stained shore.

Nobles once high-hearted,
From their homes have parted,
Scattered, scared, and started
By a base-born band.

Spots that once were cheering,
Girls beloved, endearing,
Friends from whom I'm steering,
Take this parting tear.

**Translated by Thomas Furlong**

# Celtic Speech

Never forgetful silence fall on thee,
Nor younger voices overtake thee,
Nor echoes from thine ancient hills forsake thee,
Old music heard by Mona of the sea;
And where with moving melodies there break thee,
Pastoral Conway, venerable Dee.

Like music lives, nor may that music die,
Still in the far, fair Gaelic places;
The speech, so wistful with its kindly graces,
Holy Croagh Patrick* knows, and holy Hy;
The speech, that wakes the soul in withered faces,
And wakes remembrance of great things gone by.

Like music by the desolate Land's End,
Mournful forgetfulness hath broken;
No more words kindred to the winds are spoken,
Where upon iron cliffs whole seas expend
That strength, whereof the unalterable token
Remains wild music, even to the world's end.

Lionel Johnson

*The holiest mountain in Christian Ireland

# A Grafted Tongue

(Dumb,
bloodied, the severed
head now chokes to
speak another tongue:—

As in
a long suppressed dream,
some stuttering garb-
led ordeal of my own)

An Irish
child weeps at school
repeating its English.
After each mistake

The master
gouges another mark
on the tally stick
hung about its neck

Like a bell
on a cow, a hobble
on a straying goat.
To slur and stumble

In shame
the altered syllables
of your own name;
to stray sadly home

And find
the turf cured width
of your parents' hearth
growing slowly alien:

In cabin
and field, they still
speak the old tongue.
You may greet no one.

To grow
a second tongue, as
harsh a humiliation
as twice to be born.

Decades later
that child's grandchild's
speech stumbles over lost
syllables of an old order.

John Montague

# Traditions

*for Tom Flanagan*

### I

Our guttural muse
was bulled long ago
by the alliterative tradition,
her uvula grows

vestigial, forgotten
like the coccyx
or a Brigid's Cross
yellowing in some outhouse

while custom, that 'most
sovereign mistress',
beds us down into
the British isles.

### II

We are to be proud
of our Elizabethan English:
'varsity', for example,
is grass-roots stuff with us;

we 'deem' or we 'allow'
when we suppose
and some cherished archaisms
are correct Shakespearean.

Not to speak of the furled
consonants of lowlanders
shuttling obstinately
between bawn and mossland.

### III

MacMorris, gallivanting
round the Globe, whinged
to courtier and groundling
who had heard tell of us

as going very bare
of learning, as wild hares,
as anatomies of death:
'What ish my nation?'

And sensibly, though so much
later, the wandering Bloom
replied, 'Ireland,' said Bloom,
'I was born here. Ireland.'

Seamus Heaney

# The Dream-Language of Fergus

### I

Your tongue has spent the night
In its dim sack as the shape of your foot
In its cave. Not the rudiment
Of half a vanquished sound,
The excommunicated shadow of a name,
Has rumpled the sheets of your mouth.

### II

So Latin sleeps, they say, in Russian speech,
So one river inserted into another
Becomes a leaping, glistening, splashed
And scattered alphabet
Jutting out from the voice,
Till what began as a dog's bark
Ends with bronze, what began
With honey ends with ice;
As if an aeroplane in full flight
Launched a second plane,
The sky is stabbed by their exits
And the mistaken meaning of each.

III

Conversation is as necessary
Among these families campus trees
As the apartness of torches,
And if I am a threader
Of double-stranded words, whose
Quando has grown into now,
No text can return the honey
In its path of light from a jar,
Only a seed-fund, a pendulum,
Pressing out the diasporic snow.

Medbh McGuckian

# Exile

For a people so attached to their native soil, no fate could be more terrible than exile. This fate, above all, taught Irish writers how to wring beauty from a breaking heart.

# Colum-Cille's* Farewell to Ireland

Alas for the voyage, O High King of Heaven,
Enjoined upon me,
For that I on the red plain of bloody Cooldrevin
Was present to see.

How happy the son is of Dima; no sorrow
For him is designed,
He is having, this hour, round his own hill in Durrow,
The wish of his mind.

The sounds of the winds in the elms, like strings of
A harp being played,
The note of a blackbird that claps with the wings of
Delight in the shade.

With him in Ros-Grencha the cattle are lowing
At earliest dawn,
On the brink of the summer the pigeons are cooing
And doves in the lawn.

Three things am I leaving behind me, the very
Most dear that I know,
Tir-Leedach I'm leaving, and Durrow and Derry;
Alas, I must go!

*Irish saint of the 6th century

Yet my visit and feasting with Comgall have eased me
At Cainneach's right hand,
And all but thy government, Eiré, have pleased me,
Thou waterful land.

Translated by Douglas Hyde

# A Farewell to Fál

Sad to fare from the hills of Fál,
Sad to leave the land of Ireland!
The sweet land of the bee-haunted bens,
Isle of the hoof-prints of young horses!

Albeit my faring is over the eastward ocean,
And my back is turned to the land of Fionntain,
All heart for the road hath left me:
No sod shall I love but the sod of Ireland.

Sod that is heaviest with fruit of trees,
Sod that is greenest with grassy meadows,
Old plain of Ir, dewy, crop-abounding,
The branchy wheat-bearing country!
.....................................................
If God were to grant me back again
To come to my native world,
From the Galls I would not take it to go
Among the crafty clans of England.

Were there even no peril of the sea
In leaving the lios of Laoghaire,
I shall not deny that my courage would droop—
To fare from Delvin* is hard!

*Dublin

Good-bye to the band I leave behind,
The lads of Dundargveis,
The songs and minstrelsy of the plain of Meath,
Plain of the noblest companies!

Gerald Nugent
Translated by Padraic Pearse

# The Flight of the Earls*

This night sees Eire desolate,
Her chiefs are cast out of their state;
Her men, her maidens weep to see
Her desolate that should peopled be.

How desolate is Connla's plain,
Though aliens swarm in her domain;
Her rich bright soil had joy in these
That now are scattered overseas.

Man after man, day after day
Her noblest princes pass away
And leave to all the rabble rest
A land dispeopled of her best.

O'Donnell goes. In that stern strait
Sore-stricken Ulster mourns her fate,
And all the northern shore makes moan
To hear that Aodh of Annagh's gone.

*The earls of Tyrone and Tyrconnel and their followers, who
fled to the Continent after the battle of Kinsale in 1601

Men smile at childhood's play no more,
Music and song, their day is o'er;
At wine, at Mass the kingdom's heirs
Are seen no more; changed hearts are theirs.

They feast no more, they gamble not,
All goodly pastime is forgot,
They barter not, they race no steeds,
They take no joy in stirring deeds.

No praise in builded song expressed
They hear, no tales before they rest;
None care for books and none take glee
To hear the long-traced pedigree.

The packs are silent, there's no sound
Of the old strain on Bregian ground.
A foreign flood holds all the shore,
And the great wolf-dog barks no more.

Woe to the Gael in this sore plight!
Hence forth they shall not know delight.
No tidings now their woe relieves,
Too close the gnawing sorrow cleaves.

These the examples of their woe:
Israel in Egypt long ago,
Troy that the Greek hosts set on flame,
And Babylon that to ruin came.

Sundered from hope, what friendly hand
Can save the sea-surrounded land?
The clan of Conn no Moses see
To lead them from captivity.

Her chiefs are gone. There's none to bear
Her cross or lift her from despair;
The grieving lords take ship. With these
Our very souls pass overseas.

**Translated by Robin Flower**

# The Wild Geese*

The Wild Geese—the Wild Geese—'tis long since they
   flew
O'er the billowy ocean's bright bosom of blue;
For the foot of the false-hearted stranger had curst
The shores on whose fond breast they'd settled at first;
And they sought them a home afar off o'er the sea,
Where their pinions, at least, might be chainless and free.

The Wild Geese—the Wild Geese—sad, sad was the wail
That followed their flight on the easterly gale;
But the eyes that had wept o'er their vanishing track
Ne'er brightened to welcome the wanderers back;
The home of their youth was the land of the slave,
And they died on that shore far away o'er the wave.

The Wild Geese—the Wild Geese—their coming once
   more,
Was the long-cherished hope of that desolate shore,
For the loved ones behind knew it would yet be free,
If they flew on their white pinions back o'er the sea;
But vainly the hope of these lonely ones burned,
The Wild Geese—the Wild Geese—they never returned.

*The followers of James II, who fled to France after the Battle of the Boyne,
1690

The Wild Geese—the Wild Geese—hark! heard ye
    that cry?
And marked ye that white flock o'erspreading the sky?
Can ye read not the omen? Joy, joy to the slave,
And gladness and strength to the hearts of the brave;
For Wild Geese are coming at length o'er the sea,
And Eirinn, green Eirinn, once more shall be free!

Michael Joseph Barry

# My Grief on the Sea

My grief on the sea,
　　How the waves of it roll!
For they heave between me
　　And the love of my soul!

Abandoned, forsaken,
　　To grief and to care,
Will the sea ever waken
　　Relief from despair?

My grief and my trouble!
　　Would he and I were
In the province of Leinster
　　Or the county of Clare.

Were I and my darling—
　　Oh, heart-bitter wound!—
On board of the ship
　　For America bound.

On a green bed of rushes
　　All last night I lay,
And I flung it abroad
　　With the heat of the day.

And my love came behind me—
He came from the South;
His breast to my bosom.
His mouth to my mouth.

**Translated by Douglas Hyde**

# The County Of Mayo

On the deck of Patrick Lynch's boat I sat in woeful plight,
Through my sighing all the weary day, and weeping all
  the night,
Were it not that full of sorrow from my people forth I go,
By the blessed sun! 'tis royally I'd sing thy praise, Mayo!

When I dwelt at home in plenty, and my gold did much
  abound,
In the company of fair young maids the Spanish ale went
  round—
'Tis a bitter change from those gay days that now I'm forced
  to go,
And must leave my bones in Santa Cruz, far from my
  own Mayo.

They are altered girls in Irrul now; 'tis proud they're grown
  and high,
With their hair-bags and their top-knots—for I pass their
  buckles by;
But it's little now I heed their airs, for God will have it so,
That I must depart for foreign lands, and leave my sweet
  Mayo.

'Tis my grief that Patrick Loughlinn is not Earl in Irrul still,
And that Brian Duff no longer rules as lord upon the hill;
And that Colonel Hugh MacGrady should be lying cold
    and low,
And I be sailing, sailing swiftly from the County of Mayo.

Translated by George Fox

# Siberia

In Siberia's wastes
    The Ice-wind's breath
Woundeth like the toothéd steel.
Lost Siberia doth reveal
    Only blight and death.

Blight and death alone.
    No Summer sun shines.
Night is interblent with Day
In Siberia's wastes alway
    The blood blackens, the heart pines.

In Siberia's wastes
    No tears are shed,
For they freeze within the brain.
Nought is felt but dullest pain.
    Pain acute, yet dead.

Pain as in a dream,
    When years go by
Funeral-paced, yet fugitive,
When man lives and doth not live,
    Doth not live—nor die.

In Siberia's wastes
    Are sands and rocks.
    Nothing blooms of green or soft,
    But the snow-peaks rise aloft
    And the gaunt ice-blocks.

And the exile there
    Is one with those;
    They are part and he is part,
    For the sands are in his heart,
    And the killing snows.

Therefore, in those wastes
    None curse the Czar.
    Each man's tongue is cloven by
    The North Blast, who heweth nigh
    With sharp scimitar.

And such doom each drees,*
    Till, hunger-gnawn,
    And cold-slain, he at length sinks there,
    Yet scarce more a corpse than ere
    His last breath was drawn.

                    James Clarence Mangan

*Suffers, endures

# Fabulous Journeys
## and
# Mythical Beings

The idea of enchanted lands and timeless creatures runs counter to the harsh experience of history. Are they merely a vain and distracting dream, or, as Yeats thought, the remnants of a vision slowly "perishing through the centuries"?

# from The Voyage of Bran

An ancient tree there is with blossoms,
On which birds call to the Hours.
'Tis in harmony it is their wont
To call together every Hour.

Splendors of every color glisten
Throughout the gentle-voiced plains.
Joy is known, ranked around music,
In southern Mag Argatnel*

Unknown is wailing or treachery
In the familiar cultivated land,
There is nothing rough or harsh,
But sweet music striking on the ear.

Without grief, without sorrow, without death,
Without any sickness, without debility,
That is the sign of Emain—
Uncommon is an equal marvel.

A beauty of a wondrous land,
Whose aspects are lovely,
Whose view is a fair country,
Incomparable is its haze.

**Translated by Kuno Meyer**

*The Silver-Cloud Plain

# Hy-Brasail*—The Isle of the Blest

On the ocean that hollows the rocks where ye dwell,
A shadowy land has appeared, as they tell;
Men thought it a region of sunshine and rest,
And they called it Hy-Brasail, the isle of the blest.
From year unto year on the ocean's blue rim,
The beautiful spectre showed lovely and dim;
The golden clouds curtained the deep where it lay,
And it looked like an Eden, away, far away!

A peasant who heard of the wonderful tale,
In the breeze of the Orient loosened his sail;
From Ara, the holy, he turned to the west,
For though Ara was holy, Hy-Brasail was blest.
He heard not the voices that called from the shore—
He heard not the rising wind's menacing roar;
Home, kindred, and safety he left on that day,
And he sped to Hy-Brasail, away, far away!

Morn rose on the deep, and that shadowy isle,
O'er the faint rim of distance, reflected its smile;
Noon burned on the wave, and that shadowy shore
Seemed lovelily distant, and faint as before;

*A phantom island off the west coast of Ireland

Lone evening came down on the wanderer's track,
And to Ara again he looked timidly back;
Oh, far on the verge of the ocean it lay,
Yet the isle of the blest was away, far away!

Rash dreamer, return! O, ye winds of the main,
Bear him back to his own peaceful Ara again.
Rash fool! for a vision of fanciful bliss,
To barter thy calm life of labour and peace.
The warning of reason was spoken in vain;
He never revisited Ara again!
Night fell on the deep, amidst tempest and spray,
And he died on the waters, away, far away!

Gerald Griffin

# Sailing to Byzantium

### I

That is no country for old men. The young
In one another's arms, birds in the trees,
—Those dying generations—at their song,
The salmon-falls, the mackerel-crowded seas,
Fish, flesh, or fowl, commend all summer long
Whatever is begotten, born, and dies.
Caught in that sensual music all neglect
Monuments of unageing intellect.

### II

An aged man is but a paltry thing,
A tattered coat upon a stick, unless
Soul clap its hands and sing, and louder sing
For every tatter in its mortal dress,
Nor is there singing school but studying
Monuments of its own magnificence;
And therefore I have sailed the seas and come
To the holy city of Byzantium.

### III

O sages standing in God's holy fire
As in the gold mosaic of a wall,
Come from the holy fire, perne in a gyre,
And be the singing-masters of my soul.

Consume my heart away; sick with desire
And fastened to a dying animal
It knows not what it is; and gather me
Into the artifice of eternity.

IV

Once out of nature I shall never take
My bodily form from any natural thing,
But such a form as Grecian goldsmiths make
Of hammered gold and gold enamelling
To keep a drowsy Emperor awake;
Or set upon a golden bough to sing
To lords and ladies of Byzantium
Of what is past, or passing, or to come.

William Butler Yeats

## *from* Armageddon, Armageddon

### II

When Oisin came back to Ireland
After three hundred years
On one of those enchanted islands
Somewhere in the Western Seas,

He thought nothing of dismounting
From his enchanted steed
To be one again with the mountains,
The bogs and the little fields.

There and then he began to stoop,
His hair, and all his teeth, fell out,
A mildewed belt, a rusted buckle.
The clays were heavy, black or yellow,
Those were the colours of his boots.
And I know something of how he felt.

Paul Muldoon

# The Fairy Host

Pure white the shields their arms upbear,
With silver emblems rare o'ercast;
Amid blue glittering blades they go,
The horns they blow are loud of blast.

In well-instructed ranks of war
Before their Chief they proudly pace;
Coerulean spears o'er every crest—
A curly-tressed, pale-visaged race.

Beneath the flame of their attack,
Bare and black turns every coast;
With such a terror to the fight
Flashes that mighty vengeful host.

Small wonder that their strength is great,
Since royal in estate are all,
Each hero's head a lion's fell—
A golden yellow mane lets fall.

Comely and smooth their bodies are,
Their eyes the starry blue eclipse,
The pure white crystal of their teeth
Laughs out beneath their thin red lips.

Good are they at man-slaying feats,
Melodious over meats and ale;
Of woven verse they wield the spell,
At chess-craft they excel the Gael.

Translated by Alfred Perceval Graves

# The Hosting of the Sidhe

The host is riding from Knocknarea
And over the grave of Clooth-na-bare;
Caolte tossing his burning hair
And Niamh calling *Away, come away:*
*Empty your heart of its mortal dream.*
*The winds awaken, the leaves whirl round,*
*Our cheeks are pale, our hair is unbound,*
*Our breasts are heaving, our eyes are a-gleam,*
*Our arms are waving, our lips are apart;*
*And if any gaze on our rushing band,*
*We come between him and the deed of his hand,*
*We come between him and the hope of his heart.*
The host is rushing 'twixt night and day,
And where is there hope or deed as fair?
Caolte tossing his burning hair,
And Niamh calling *Away, come away.*

William Butler Yeats

# The Passing of the Shee

Adieu, sweet Angus, Maeve, and Fand,
Ye plumed yet skinny Shee,
That poets played with hand in hand
To learn their ecstasy.

We'll stretch in Red Dan Sally's ditch,
And drink in Tubber fair,
Or poach with Red Dan Philly's bitch
The badger and the hare.

John Millington Synge

# Requiems

Few peoples have experienced as many military and political reversals as the Irish. To transform the bitterness of despair has been the task of the Irish requiem.

# Requiem for the Croppies*

The pockets of our great coats full of barley—
No kitchens on the run, no striking camp—
We moved quick and sudden in our own country.
The priest lay behind ditches with the tramp.
A people, hardly marching—on the hike—
We found new tactics happening each day:
We'd cut through reins and rider with the pike
And stampede cattle into infantry,
Then retreat through hedges where cavalry must be thrown.
Until, on Vinegar Hill, the fatal conclave.
Terraced thousands died, shaking scythes at cannon.
The hillside blushed, soaked in our broken wave.
They buried us without shroud or coffin
And in August the barley grew up out of the grave.

Seamus Heaney

*Young Irish rebels of 1798, so named for their close-cropped hair

# Lament for the Death of Eoghan Ruadh O'Neill*

'Did they dare, did they dare, to slay Owen Roe O'Neill?'
'Yes, they slew with poison him they feared to meet with
    steel.'
'May God wither up their hearts! May their blood cease to
    flow!
May they walk in living death, who poisoned Owen Roe!

'Though it break my heart to hear, say again the bitter
    words.'
'From Derry, against Cromwell, he marched to measure
    swords;
But the weapon of the Saxon met him on his way,
And he died at Cloc Uactair, upon Saint Leonard's Day.'

'Wail, wail ye for the Mighty One! Wail, wail ye for the
    Dead!
Quench the hearth, and hold the breath—with ashes strew
    the head!
How tenderly we loved him! How deeply we deplore!
Holy Saviour! but to think we shall never see him more!

*An Irish leader in the War of the Forties (17th century). Popular tradition
had it that he was poisoned by the English.

'Sagest in the council was he, kindest in the hall:
Sure we never won a battle—'twas Owen won them all.
Had he lived, had he lived, our dear country had been free;
But he's dead, but he's dead, and 'tis slaves we'll ever be.

'O'Farrell and Clanrickarde, Preston and Red Hugh,
Audley and MacMahon, ye are valiant, wise, and true;
But what—what are ye all to our darling who is gone?
The rudder of our ship was he—our castle's corner-stone!

'Wail, wail him through the island! Weep, weep for our
     pride!
Would that on the battle-field our gallant chief had died!
Weep the Victor of Beinn Burb—weep him, young men
     and old!
Weep for him, ye women—your Beautiful lies cold!

'We thought you would not die—we were sure you would
     not go,
And leave us in our utmost need to Cromwell's cruel
     blow—
Sheep without a shepherd, when the snow shuts out the
     sky—
Oh! why did you leave us, Owen? why did you die?

'Soft as woman's was your voice, O'Neill! bright was
    your eye!
Oh! why did you leave us, Owen? why did you die?
Your troubles are all over—you're at rest with God on high;
But we're slaves, and we're orphans, Owen!—why did
    you die?'

Thomas Osborne Davis

# The Flight of the Earls

> This was a distinguished crew for one
> ship; for it is indeed certain that the
> sea had not supported, and the winds
> had not wafted from Ireland, in
> modern times, a party of one ship
> who would have been more illustrious,
> or noble in point of genealogy, or
> more renowned for deeds, valour or
> high achievements....
> *Annals of the Four Masters*

The fiddler settles in
to his playing so easily;
rosewood box tucked under chin,
saw of rosined bow
& angle of elbow

that the mind elides
for a while what he plays:
hornpipe or reel to warm
us up well, heel to toecap
twitching in tune

till the sound expands
in the slow climb of a lament.
As by some forest campfire
listeners draw near, to honour
a communal loss

& a shattered procession
of anonymous suffering
files through the brain:
burnt houses, pillaged farms,
a province in flames.

We have killed, burnt and despoiled
all along the Lough to within four
miles of Dungannon...in which
journeys we have killed above a
hundred of all sorts, besides such as
we have burned, how many I know
not. We spare none, of what quality or
sex soever, and it had bred much
terror in the people who heard not a
drum nor saw not a fire of long time.
*Chichester to Mountjoy, Spring 1601*

With an intricate
& mournful mastery
the thin bow glides & slides,
assuaging like a bardic poem,
our tribal pain—

> *Is uaigneach Eire*

Disappearance & death
of a world, as down Lough Swilly
the great ship, encumbered with nobles,
swells its sails for Europe:

The Flight of the Earls.

John Montague

# The Memory of the Dead

Who fears to speak of Ninety-Eight?*
    Who blushes at the name?
When cowards mock the patriot's fate,
    Who hangs his head for shame?
He's all a knave, or half a slave,
    Who slights his country thus;
But a true man, like you, man,
    Will fill your glass with us.

We drink the memory of the brave,
    The faithful and the few:
Some lie far off beyond the wave,
    Some sleep in Ireland, too;
All, all are gone; but still lives on
    The fame of those who died;
All true men, like you, men,
    Remember them with pride.

Some on the shores of distant lands
    Their weary hearts have laid,
And by the stranger's heedless hands
    Their lonely graves were made;

*The uprising of 1798. The men of '98 were Wolf Tone, the
Sheares brothers, Lord Edward, Father John Murphy, and others
who died in that failed rebellion.

But, though their clay be far away
    Beyond the Atlantic foam,
In true men, like you, men,
    Their spirit's still at home.

The dust of some is Irish earth,
    Among their own they rest,
And the same land that gave them birth
    Has caught them to her breast;
And we will pray that from their clay
    Full many a race may start
Of true men, like you, men,
    To act as brave a part.

They rose in dark and evil days
    To right their native land;
They kindled here a living blaze
    That nothing shall withstand.
Alas! that Might can vanquish Right—
    They fell and passed away;
But true men, like you, men,
    Are plenty here to-day.

Then here's their memory—may it be
    For us a guiding light,
To cheer our strife for liberty,
    And teach us to unite—

Through good and ill, be Ireland's still,
   Though sad as theirs your fate,
And true men be you, men,
   Like those of Ninety-Eight.

John Kells Ingram

# The Burial of Sir John Moore

Not a drum was heard, not a funeral note,
　　As his corse to the rampart we hurried;
Not a soldier discharged his farewell shot
　　O'er the grave where our hero we buried.

We buried him darkly at dead of night,
　　The sods with our bayonets turning,
By the struggling moonbeam's misty light,
　　And the lantern dimly burning.

No useless coffin enclosed his breast,
　　Not in sheet or in shroud we wound him;
But he lay like a warrior taking his rest,
　　With his martial cloak around him.

Few and short were the prayers we said,
　　And we spoke not a word of sorrow;
But we steadfastly gazed on the face that was dead,
　　And we bitterly thought of the morrow.

We thought as we hollow'd his narrow bed,
　　And smooth'd down his lonely pillow,
That the foe and the stranger would tread o'er his
　　　　head
　　And we far away on the billow!

Lightly they'll talk of the spirit that's gone,
    And o'er his cold ashes upbraid him,—
But little he'll reck, if they let him sleep on
    In the grave where a Briton has laid him.

But half of our heavy task was done,
    When the clock struck the hour for retiring;
And we heard the distant and random gun
    That the foe was silently firing.

Slowly and sadly we laid him down,
    From the field of his fame fresh and gory;
We carved not a line, and we raised not a stone—
    But we left him alone in his glory!

Charles Wolfe

# Lament for Thomas MacDonagh

He shall not hear the bittern cry
In the wild sky, where he is lain,
Nor voices of the sweeter birds
Above the wailing of the rain.

Nor shall he know when loud March blows
Thro' slanting snows her fanfare shrill,
Blowing to flame the golden cup
Of many an upset daffodil.

But when the Dark Cow leaves the moor,
And pastures poor with greedy weeds,
Perhaps he'll hear her low at morn
Lifting her horn in pleasant meads.

Francis Ledwidge

# Easter, 1916

I have met them at close of day
Coming with vivid faces
From counter or desk among grey
Eighteenth-century houses.
I have passed with a nod of the head
Or polite meaningless words,
Or have lingered awhile and said
Polite meaningless words,
And thought before I had done
Of a mocking tale or a gibe
To please a companion
Around the fire at the club,
Being certain that they and I -
But lived where motley is worn:
All changed, changed utterly:
A terrible beauty is born.

That woman's days were spent
In ignorant good will,
Her nights in argument
Until her voice grew shrill.
What voice more sweet than hers
When young and beautiful,
She rode to harriers?

This man had kept a school
And rode our winged horse;
This other his helper and friend
Was coming into his force;
He might have won fame in the end,
So sensitive his nature seemed,
So daring and sweet his thought.
This other man I had dreamed
A drunken, vain-glorious lout.
He had done most bitter wrong
To some who are near my heart,
Yet I number him in the song;
He, too, has resigned his part
In the casual comedy;
He, too, has been changed in his turn,
Transformed utterly:
A terrible beauty is born.

Hearts with one purpose alone
Through summer and winter seem
Enchanted to a stone
To trouble the living stream.
The horse that comes from the road,
The rider, the birds that range
From cloud to tumbling cloud,
Minute by minute change;
A shadow of cloud on the stream

Changes minute by minute;
A horse-hoof slides on the brim,
And a horse plashes within it
Where long-legged moor-hens dive,
And hens to moor-cocks call.
Minute by minute they live:
The stone's in the midst of all.

Too long a sacrifice
Can make a stone of the heart.
O when may it suffice?
That is heaven's part, our part
To murmur name upon name,
As a mother names her child
When sleep at last has come
On limbs that had run wild.
What is it but nightfall?
No, no, not night but death;
Was it needless death after all?
For England may keep faith
For all that is done and said.
We know their dream; enough
To know they dreamed and are dead.
And what if excess of love
Bewildered them till they died?
I write it out in a verse—

MacDonagh and MacBride
And Connolly and Pearse
Now and in time to be,
Wherever green is worn,
Are changed, changed utterly:
A terrible beauty is born.

William Butler Yeats

# Tender Love

**F**rom witty music hall song to sentimental Victorian verse to the grave lyrics of Yeats and Joyce who pursued "the old high way of love," Irish poetry continually returns to a single theme: the saving grace of love.

# Eileen Aroon*

When, like the early rose,
        Eileen aroon!
Beauty in childhood blows,
        Eileen aroon!
When, like a diadem,
Buds blush around the stem,
Which is the fairest gem?
        Eileen aroon!

Is it the laughing eye,
        Eileen aroon!
Is it the timid sigh?
        Eileen aroon!
Is it the tender tone,
Soft as the stringed harp's moan?
Oh! it is Truth alone,
        Eileen aroon!

When, like the rising day,
        Eileen aroon!
Love sends his early ray,
        Eileen aroon!

*Eileen, my treasure

What makes his dawning glow
Changeless through joy or woe?
Only the constant know—
      Eileen aroon!

I know a valley fair,
      Eileen aroon!
I knew a cottage there,
      Eileen aroon!
Far in that valley's shade
I knew a gentle maid,
Flower of a hazel glade,
      Eileen aroon!

Who in the song so sweet?
      Eileen aroon!
Who in the dance so fleet?
      Eileen aroon!
Dear were her charms to me,
Dearer her laughter free,
Dearest her constancy,
      Eileen aroon!

Were she no longer true,
      Eileen aroon!
What should her lover do?
      Eileen aroon!

Fly with his broken chain
Far o'er the sounding main,
Never to love again,
Eileen aroon!

Youth must with time decay,
Eileen aroon!
Beauty must fade away,
Eileen aroon!
Castles are sacked in war,
Chieftains are scattered far,
Truth is a fixéd star,
Eileen aroon!

Gerald Griffin

# Labasheedy (The Silken Bed)

I'd make a bed for you
in Labasheedy
in the tall grass
under the wrestling trees
where your skin
would be silk upon silk
in the darkness
when the moths are coming down.

Skin which glistens
shining over your limbs
like milk being poured
from jugs at dinnertime;
your hair is a herd of goats
moving over rolling hills,
hills that have high cliffs
and two ravines.

And your damp lips
would be as sweet as sugar
at evening and we walking
by the riverside

with honeyed breezes
blowing over the Shannon
and the fuchsias bowing down to you
one by one.

The fuchsias bending low
their solemn heads
in obeisance to the beauty
in front of them
I would pick a pair of flowers
as pendant earrings
to adorn you
like a bride in shining clothes.

O I'd make a bed for you
in Labasheedy,
in the twilight hour
with evening falling slow
and what a pleasure it would be
to have our limbs entwine
wrestling
while the moths are coming down.

Nuala Ní Dhomhnaill
Translated by the author

# Cashel of Munster

I'd wed you without herds, without money, or rich array,
And I'd wed you on a dewy morning at daydawn grey;
My bitter woe it is, love, that we are not far away
In Cashel town, though the bare deal board were our
    marriage-bed this day!

O, fair maid, remember the green hill side,
Remember how I hunted about the valleys wide;
Time now has worn me; my locks are turned to grey,
The year is scarce and I am poor, but send me not, love,
    away!

O, deem not my blood is of base strain, my girl,
O, deem not my birth was as the birth of the churl;
Marry me, and prove me, and say soon you will,
That noble blood is written on my right side still!

My purse holds no red gold, no coin of the silver white,
No herds are mine to drive through the long twilight!
But the pretty girl that would take me, all bare though I be
    and lone,
O, I'd take her with me kindly to the county Tyrone.

O, my girl I can see 'tis in trouble you are,
And, O, my girl, I see 'tis your people's reproach you bear:
"I am a girl in trouble for his sake with whom I fly,
And, O, may no other maiden know such reproach as I!"

Translated by Samuel Ferguson

# The Low-Backed Car

When first I saw sweet Peggy,
    'Twas on a market day,
A low-backed car she drove, and sat
    Upon a truss of hay;
But when that hay was blooming grass,
    And decked with flowers of Spring,
No flow'r was there that could compare
    With the blooming girl I sing.
As she sat in the low-backed car—
The man at the turnpike bar
    Never asked for the toll,
    But just rubbed his ould poll
And looked after the low-backed car.

In battle's wild commotion,
    The proud and mighty Mars,
With hostile scythes, demands his tithes
    Of death—in warlike cars;
While Peggy, peaceful goddess,
    Has darts in her bright eye,
That knock men down, in the market town,
    As right and left they fly—
While she sits in her low-backed car,

Than battle more dangerous far—
    For the doctor's art
    Cannot cure the heart
That is hit from that low-backed car.

Sweet Peggy, round her car, sir,
    Has strings of ducks and geese,
But the scores of hearts she slaughters
    By far outnumber these;
While she among her poultry sits,
    Just like a turtle-dove,
Well worth the cage, I do engage,
    Of the blooming god of love!
While she sits in her low-backed car
The lovers come near and far,
    And envy the chicken
    That Peggy is pickin'
As she sits in the low-backed car.

Oh, I'd rather own that car, sir,
    With Peggy by my side,
Than a coach-and-four and goold galore,
    And a lady for my bride;
For the lady would sit forninst* me,
    On a cushion made with taste,

*Against

While Peggy would sit beside me
   With my arm around her waist—
While we drove in the low-backed car,
To be married by Father Maher,
   Oh, my heart would beat high
   At her glance and her sigh—
Though it beat in a low-backed car.

Samuel Lover

# A Love Song

He is a heart,
An acorn from the oakwood.
He is young.
A kiss for him!

**7th or 8th century**
**Translated by Myles Dillon**

# Down by the Salley Gardens

Down by the salley gardens my love and I did meet;
She passed the salley gardens with little snow-white feet.
She bid me take love easy, as the leaves grow on the tree;
But I, being young and foolish, with her would not agree.

In a field by the river my love and I did stand,
And on my leaning shoulder she laid her snow-white hand.
She bid me take life easy, as the grass grows on the weirs;
But I was young and foolish, and now am full of tears.

William Butler Yeats

# *from* Chamber Music

### I

Strings in the earth and air
   Make music sweet;
Strings by the river where
   The willows meet.

There's music along the river
   For Love wanders there,
Pale flowers on his mantle,
   Dark leaves on his hair.

All softly playing,
   With head to the music bent,
And fingers straying
   Upon an instrument.

James Joyce

# Fatal Love

$\mathcal{Y}$eats writes that "love was held to be a fatal sickness in ancient Ireland," and this belief has survived. Loss of heart, loss of soul, loss of life: these are the consequences of fatal love.

# The Love-Talker

I met the Love-Talker one eve in the glen,
He was handsomer than any of our handsome young men,
His eyes were blacker than the sloe, his voice sweeter far
Than the crooning of old Kevin's pipes beyond in
    Coolnagar.

I was bound for the milking with a heart fair and free—
My grief! my grief! that bitter hour drained the life from me;
I thought him human lover, though his lips on mine were
    cold,
And the breath of death blew keen on me within his hold.

I know not what way he came, no shadow fell behind,
But all the sighing rushes swayed beneath a faery wind
The thrush ceased its singing, a mist crept about,
We two clung together—with the world shut out.

Beyond the ghostly mist I could hear my cattle low,
The little cow from Ballina, clean as driven snow,
The dun cow from Kerry, the roan from Inisheer,
Oh, pitiful their calling—and his whispers in my ear!

His eyes were a fire; his words were a snare;
I cried my mother's name, but no help was there;
I made the blessed Sign; then he gave a dreary moan,
A wisp of cloud went floating by, and I stood alone.

Running ever through my head, is an old-time rune—
"Who meets the Love-Talker must weave her shroud
     soon."
My mother's face is furrowed with the salt tears that fall,
But the kind eyes of my father are the saddest sight of all.

I have spun the fleecy lint, and now my wheel is still,
The linen length is woven for my shroud fine and chill,
I shall stretch me on the bed where a happy maid I lay—
Pray for the soul of Mairé Og at dawning of the day!

Ethna Carbery

# He Charges Her to Lay Aside Her Weapons

I charge you, lady young and fair,
    Straightway to lay your arms aside.
Lay by your armour, would you dare
    To spread the slaughter far and wide?

O lady, lay your armour by,
    Conceal your curling hair also,
For never was a man could fly
    The coils that o'er your bosom flow.

And if you answer, lady fair,
    That north or south you ne'er took life,
Your very eyes, your glance, your air
    Can murder without axe or knife.

And oh! If you but bare your knee,
    If you your soft hand's palm advance,
You'll slaughter many a company.
    What more is done with shield and lance?

Oh, hide your bosom limey white,
    Your naked side conceal from me.
Ah, show them not in all men's sight,
    Your breasts more bright than flowering tree.

And if in you there's shame or fear
    For all the murders you have done,
Let those bright eyes no more appear,
    Those shining teeth be seen of none.

Lady, we tremble far and near!
    Be with these conquests satisfied,
And lest I perish, lady dear,
    Oh, lay those arms of yours aside.

Pierce Ferriter
Translated by the Earl of Longford

# *from* Donal Oge: Grief of a Girl's Heart

My heart is as black as the blackness of the sloe,
Or as the black coal that is on the smith's forge;
Or as the sole of a shoe left in white halls;
It was you put that darkness over my life.

You have taken the east from me; you have taken the west
  from me,
You have taken what is before me and what is behind me;
You have taken the moon, you have taken the sun from me,
And my fear is great that you have taken God from me!

**Translated by Lady Gregory**

# I Shall Not Die for Thee

For thee I shall not die,
        Woman high of fame and name;
Foolish men thou mayest slay,
        I and they are not the same.

Why should I expire
        For the fire of any eye,
Slender waist or swan-like limb,
        Is't for them that I should die?

The round breasts, the fresh skin,
        Cheeks crimson, hair so long and rich;
Indeed, indeed, I shall not die,
        Please God, not I, for any such.

The golden hair, the forehead then,
        The chaste mien, the gracious ease,
The rounded heel, the languid tone,
        Fools alone find death from these.

Thy sharp wit, thy perfect calm,
        Thy thin palm like foam of sea;
Thy white neck, thy blue eye,
        I shall not die for thee.

Woman, graceful as the swan,
    A wise man did nurture me,
Little palm, white neck, bright eye,
    I shall not die for thee.

**Translated by Douglas Hyde**

# Fair Cassidy

I left my prayers and the kneeling pilgrims
And went wild running down the holy Reek*
And all who saw me said: 'That is Cassidy
Who abandoned God for a girl's cheek.'

The first time I saw her I was a student
Reading my prayerbook, I raised my eyes
But they betrayed me, raced to embrace her,
And I had not slept at the next sunrise.

When I was at College they taught me English
And praised my accent, but with that first sight
The only language that I knew was love-talk
And all my thoughts were turned to birds in flight.

I have no land, no stock nor money
To win that girl to me, I cannot pray,
But I'd mount the Reek on my bleeding knees
If I could have her on my wedding-day.

She could cheat my heart to believe in marvels,
That no grass would grow, that no moon would shine,
That the stars are lightless, that she could love me;
And oh! Christ in Heaven that she were mine.

*Also known as Croagh Patrick (see footnote p. 20)

The sun will cool and the moon will darken
And fishes swim in an empty sea,
The floods will rise above the mountains
And Cassidy still be in slavery.

She passes by and I curse the mother
Who bore that daughter to torture me—
Ah sweet, if we could elope together
I'd risk my neck on the gallows tree.

There is no hill and there's no valley,
No road, no bog that she passes by
But is filled with music, heart-breaking music,
And may Christ have mercy on Cassidy.

**Translated by Donagh MacDonagh**

# No Second Troy

Why should I blame her that she filled my days
With misery, or that she would of late
Have taught to ignorant men most violent ways,
Or hurled the little streets upon the great,
Had they but courage equal to desire?
What could have made her peaceful with a mind
That nobleness made simple as a fire,
With beauty like a tightened bow, a kind
That is not natural in an age like this,
Being high and solitary and most stern?
Why, what could she have done being what she is?
Was there another Troy for her to burn?

William Butler Yeats

# *from* Chamber Music

## XXXVI

I hear an army charging upon the land,
    And the thunder of horses plunging, foam about their
        knees:
Arrogant, in black armour, behind them stand,
    Disdaining the reins, with fluttering whips, the
        charioteers.

They cry unto the night their battle-name:
    I moan in sleep when I hear afar their whirling laughter.
They cleave the gloom of dreams, a blinding flame,
    Clanging, clanging upon the heart as upon an anvil.

They come shaking in triumph their long, green hair:
    They come out of the sea and run shouting by the shore.
My heart, have you no wisdom thus to despair?
    My love, my love, my love, why have you left me alone?

James Joyce

# High Times
## and
# Rakish Delights

The caricature of the bluff, hard-drinking "Stage Irishman" has become repugnant as a national type. Yet these bold celebrations of the flesh make no apologies.

# from The Description of an *Irish-Feast*

*translated almost literally out of the Original* Irish

O Rourk's noble Fare
    Will ne'er be forgot,
By those who were there,
    Or those who were not.
His Revels to keep,
    We sup and we dine,
On seven Score Sheep,
    Fat Bullocks and Swine.
*Usquebagh**\* to our Feast
    In Pails was brought up,
An Hundred at least,
    And a Madder† our Cup.
O there is the Sport,
    We rise with the Light,
In disorderly Sort,
    From snoring all Night....
Come, Harper, strike up,
    But first by your Favour,
Boy, give us a Cup;
    Ay, this has some Savour:
O *Rourk*'s jolly Boys

\*Whiskey
†Wooden vessel

Ne'er dream't of the Matter,
Till rowz'd by the Noise,
And musical Clatter,
They bounce from their Nest,
No longer will tarry,
They rise ready drest,
Without one *Ave Mary.*
They dance in a Round,
Cutting Capers and Ramping,
A Mercy the Ground
Did not burst with their stamping.
The Floor is all wet
With Leaps and with Jumps,
While the Water and Sweat,
Splish, splash in their Pumps....
Good Lord, what a Sight,
After all their good Cheer,
For People to fight
In the Midst of their Beer:
They rise from their Feast,
And hot are their Brains,
A Cubit at least
The Length of their Skeans.*
What Stabs and what Cuts,

*Daggers

What clatt'ring of Sticks,
What Strokes on the Guts,
    What Bastings and Kicks!
With Cudgels of Oak,
    Well harden'd in Flame,
An hundred Heads broke,
    An hundred struck lame.
You Churle, I'll maintain
    My Father built *Lusk*,
The Castle of *Slain*,
    And *Carrickdrumrusk*:
The Earl of *Kildare*,
    And *Moynalta*, his Brother,
As great as they are,
    I was nurs'd by their Mother.
Ask that of old *Madam*,
    She'll tell you who's who,
As far up as *Adam*,
    She knows it is true,
Come down with that Beam,
    If Cudgels are scarce,
A Blow on the Weam,*
    Or a Kick on the Arse.

Jonathan Swift

*Belly

# The Rakes of Mallow

Beauing, belle-ing, dancing, drinking,
Breaking windows, damning, sinking,*
Ever raking, never thinking,
      Live the rakes of Mallow.

Spending faster than it comes,
Beating waiters, bailiffs, duns,
Bacchus's true-begotten sons,
      Live the rakes of Mallow.

One time nought but claret drinking,
Then like politicians thinking
To raise the sinking funds when sinking,
      Live the rakes of Mallow.

When at home with dadda dying,
Still for Mallow water crying;
But where there's good claret plying,
      Live the rakes of Mallow.

Living short but merry lives;
Going where the devil drives;
Having sweethearts, but no wives,
      Live the rakes of Mallow.

*Damning you to hell and then sinking you lower

Racking tenants, stewards teasing,
Swiftly spending, slowly raising,
Wishing to spend all their days in
Raking as at Mallow.

Then to end this raking life
They get sober, take a wife,
Ever after live in strife,
And wish again for Mallow.

Anonymous

## *from* The Cruiskeen Lawn*

Let the farmer praise his grounds,
Let the huntsman praise his hounds,
    The shepherd his dew-scented lawn;
But I, more blest than they,
Spend each happy night and day
    With my charming little cruiskeen lawn, lawn, lawn,
    My charming little cruiskeen lawn.
        Gra ma chree ma cruiskeen,
        Slainté geal mavourneen,
          's gra machree a cooleen bawn....

Immortal and divine,
Great Bacchus, god of wine,
    Create me by adoption your son;
In hope that you'll comply
My glass shall ne'er run dry,
    Nor my smiling little cruiskeen lawn, etc.

---

*An Cruscín Lán: Irish for "the little full jug." The English for the refrain is

    *The love of my heart is my little jug,—*
    *Bright health to my darling!*
    *The love of my heart is her fair hair.*

And when grim death appears,
In a few but pleasant years,
    To tell me that my glass has run;
I'll say, Begone, you knave,
For bold Bacchus gave me leave,
    To take another cruiskeen lawn, etc.

Then fill your glasses high,
Let's not part with lips a-dry,
    Though the lark now proclaims it is dawn;
And since we can't remain,
May we shortly meet again,
    To fill another cruiskeen lawn, etc.

Anonymous

# from The Humours of
# Donnybrook Fair*

To Donnybrook steer, all you sons of Parnassus—
    Poor painters, poor poets, poor newsmen, and knaves,
To see what the fun is, that all fun surpasses—
    The sorrow and sadness of green Erin's slaves.
Oh, Donnybrook, jewel! full of mirth is your quiver,
    Where all flock from Dublin to gape and to stare
At two elegant bridges, without e'er a river:
    So, success to the humours of Donnybrook Fair!

O you lads that are witty, from famed Dublin city,
    And you that in pastime take any delight,
To Donnybrook fly, for the time's drawing nigh
    When fat pigs are hunted, and lean cobblers fight;
When maidens, so swift, run for a new shift;
    Men, muffled in sacks, for a shirt they race there;
There jockeys well booted, and horses sure-footed,
    All keep up the humours of Donnybrook Fair....

*A Dublin fair held in August, which was discontinued because of the
fighting—hence the word "donnybrook"

Brisk lads and young lasses can there fill their glasses
    With whisky, and send a full bumper around;
Jig it off in a tent till their money's all spent,
    And spin like a top till they rest on the ground.
Oh, Donnybrook capers, to sweet catgut-scrapers,
    They bother the vapours, and drive away care;
And what is more glorious—there's naught more
      uproarious—
    Huzza for the humours of Donnybrook Fair!

                           Anonymous

# The Influence of Natural Objects

## for Bill Ireland

Night after night from our camp on Sugar Loaf Hill
We strolled the streets, roaring or quiet, daring
Anything for girls or drink, but not caring
When the town closed. We reeled home and were ill,
Cooked fries, fell senseless in our socks
On grass or blankets. I woke cold at dawn
And stumbled to the Hill Top Zoo, and on
Through pines to the bare summit's litter of rocks.
I was always scared by the huge spaces below,
Between sky and water, explosive bright air
Glinting on live-wire nerves of mine, worn bare.
I lay down, grinning, stiff with vertigo.

This roused an appetite for breakfast, bars,
Bathing, chasing the daft holiday bitches,
For jokes and poems, beer and sandwiches...
And so on till we slept under the stars.

James Simmons

# Mable Kelly

Lucky the husband
Who puts his hand beneath her head.
    They kiss without scandal
Happiest two near feather-bed.
He sees the tumble of brown hair
Unplait, the breasts, pointed and bare
    When nightdress shows
    From dimple to toe-nail,
All Mable glowing in it, here, there, everywhere.

    Music might listen
    To her least whisper,
Learn every note, for all are true.
    While she is speaking,
    Her voice goes sweetly
To charm the herons in their musing.
Her eyes are modest, blue, their darkness
Small rooms of thought, but when they sparkle
    Upon a feast-day,
    Glasses are meeting,
Each raised to Mable Kelly, our toast and darling.

Gone now are many Irish ladies
Who kissed and fondled, their very pet-names
Forgotten, their tibia degraded.
She takes their sky. Her smile is famed.
Her praise is scored by quill and pencil.
    Harp and spinet
    Are in her debt
And when she plays or sings, melody is content.

    No man who sees her
    Will feel uneasy.
He goes his way, head high, however tired.
    Lamp loses light
    When placed beside her.
She is the pearl and being of all Ireland
Foot, hand, eye, mouth, breast, thigh and instep, all that
        we desire.
Tresses that pass small curls as if to touch the ground;
    So many prizes
    Are not divided.
Her beauty is her own and she is not proud.

Turlough O'Carolan
Translated by Austin Clarke

# Nude

The long and short
of it is I'd far rather see you nude—
your silk shirt
and natty

tie, the brolly under your oxter
in case of a rainy day,
the three-piece seersucker
suit that's so incredibly trendy,

your snazzy loafers
and, la-di-da,
a pair of gloves
made from the skin of a doe,

then, to top it all, a crombie hat
set at a rak-
ish angle—none of these add
up to more than icing on the cake.

For, unbeknownst to the rest
of the world, behind the outward
show lies a body unsurpassed
for beauty, without so much as a wart

or blemish, but the brill-
iant slink of a wild animal, a dream-
cat, say, on the prowl,
leaving murder and mayhem

in its wake. Your broad, sinewy
shoulders and your flank
smooth as the snow
on a snow-bank.

Your back, your slender waist,
and, of course,
the root that is the very seat
of pleasure, the pleasure-source.

Your skin so dark, my beloved,
and soft
as silk with a hint of velvet
in its weft,

smelling as it does of meadowsweet
or 'watermead'
that has the power, or so it's said,
to drive men and women mad.

For that reason alone, if for no other,
when you come with me to the dance tonight
(though, as you know, I'd much prefer
to see you nude)

it would probably be best
for you to pull on your pants and vest
rather than send
half the women of Ireland totally round the bend.

Nuala Ní Dhomhnaill
Translated by Paul Muldoon

# Curses

The power to curse has long been a prerogative of the Irish bard. More often than not it was used to avenge a personal slight or a breach in the laws of hospitality. Its effects were believed to be real.

# A Curse on a Closed Gate

Be this the fate
Of the man who would shut his gate
On the stranger; gentle or simple, early or late.

When his mouth with a day's long hunger and thirst
 would wish
For the savour of salted fish,
Let him sit and eat his fill of an empty dish.

To the man of that ilk,
Let water stand in his churn, instead of milk
That turns a calf's coat silk.

And under the gloomy night
May never a thatch made tight
Shut out the clouds from his sight.

Above the ground or below it,
Good cheer, may he never know it,
Nor a tale by the fire, nor a dance on the road, nor a song
 by a wandering poet.

Till he open his gate
To the stranger, early or late,
And turn back the stone of his fate.

Translated by James H. Cousins

# *from* Bruadar and Smith and Glinn

Bruadar and Smith and Glinn
  Amen, dear God, I pray,
May they lie low in waves of woe,
  And tortures slow each day!
                    Amen!...

Bruadar and Smith and Glinn
  May flails of sorrow flay!
Cause for lamenting, snares and cares
  Be theirs for night and day!
                    Amen!...

For Bruadar gape the grave,
  Up-shovel for Smith the mould,
Amen, O King of the Sunday! Leave
  Glinn in the Devil's hold.
                    Amen!...

Glinn in a shaking ague,
  Cancer on Bruadar's tongue,
Amen, O King of the Heavens! and Smith
  Forever stricken dumb.
                    Amen!...

Smith like a sieve of holes,
　　Bruadar with throat decay,
Amen, O King of the Orders, Glinn
　　A buck-show every day.
　　　　　　　　　　　Amen!

Hell-hounds to hunt for Smith,
　　Glinn led to hang on high,
Amen, O King of the Judgement Day!
　　And Bruadar rotting by.
　　　　　　　　　　　Amen!...

May none of their race survive,
　　May God destroy them all,
Each curse of the psalms in the holy books
　　Of the prophets upon them fall.
　　　　　　　　　　　Amen!

Blight skull, and ear, and skin,
　　And hearing, and voice, and sight,
Amen! before the year be out,
　　Blight, Son of the Virgin, blight.
　　　　　　　　　　　Amen!

May my curses hot and red
And all I have said this day,
Strike the Black Peeler* too,
Amen! dear God, I pray!
Amen!

**Translated by Douglas Hyde**

*Policeman

# from The Curse of Doneraile

Alas! how dismal is my tale,
I lost my watch in Doneraile.
My Dublin watch, my chain and seal,
Pilfered at once in Doneraile.
May Fire and Brimstone never fail,
To fall in showers on Doneraile.
May all the leading fiends assail,
The thieving town of Doneraile,
As lightnings flash across the vale,
So down to Hell with Doneraile.
The fate of Pompey at Pharsale,
Be that the curse of Doneraile.
May Beef, or Mutton, Lamb or Veal
Be never found in Doneraile.
But Garlic Soup and scurvy Kale,
Be still the food for Doneraile.
And forward as the creeping snail,
Th' industry be, of Doneraile....
May ev'ry churn and milking pail,
Fall dry to staves in Doneraile.
May cold and hunger still congeal,
The stagnant blood of Doneraile.
May ev'ry hour new woes reveal,

That Hell reserves for Doneraile.
May ev'ry chosen ill prevail,
O'er all the Imps of Doneraile.
May no one wish or prayer avail,
To soothe the woes of Doneraile.
May th' Inquisition straight impale,
The rapparees of Doneraile.
May curse of Sodom now prevail,
And sink to ashes Doneraile.
May Charon's Boat triumphant sail,
Completely manned from Doneraile.
Oh! may my Couplets never fail,
To find new curse for Doneraile.
And may Grim Pluto's inner jail,
For ever groan with Doneraile.*

Patrick O'Kelly

*Lady Doneraile replaced O'Kelly's lost watch to take away
the curse. O'Kelly then wrote ''Blessings on Doneraile.''

# Righteous Anger

The lanky hank of a she in the inn over there
Nearly killed me for asking the loan of a glass of beer:
May the devil grip the whey-faced slut by the hair,
And beat bad manners out of her skin for a year.

That parboiled imp, with the hardest jaw you will see
On virtue's path, and a voice that would rasp the dead,
Came roaring and raging the minute she looked on me,
And threw me out of the house on the back of my head!

If I asked her master he'd give me a cask a day;
But she, with the beer at hand, not a gill would arrange!
May she marry a ghost and bear him a kitten, and may
The High King of Glory permit her to get the mange.

James Stephens

## *from* Skin the Goat's Curse on Carey*

**B**efore I set sail, I will not fail
　　To give that lad my blessing,
And if I had him here there's not much fear
　　But he'd get a good top dressing;
By the hat on my head but he'd lie on his bed
　　Till the end of next September,
I'd give him good cause to rub his jaws
　　And Skin the Goat remember.

But as I won't get the chance to make Carey dance,
　　I'll give him my benedictions,
So from my heart's core may he evermore
　　Know nothing but afflictions,
May every buck flea from here to Bray
　　Jump through the bed that he lies on,
And by some mistake may he shortly take
　　A flowing pint of poison....

May his wife be jealous and pitch up the bellows,
　　And measure him over the head,
May he get the Devil's fright, that will turn him left and
　　　　right,

*Skin the Goat participated in the Phoenix Park murders (May 6, 1882).
James Carey turned queen's evidence against his accomplices.

Every night till it knocks him stone dead,
May a horrid baboon jump out of the moon
    And tear his old carcase asunder,
And the day he'll sail, may snow and hail
    Accompany rain and thunder....

When the equator is crossed, may the rudder be lost,
    And his vessel be wafted ashore,
To some cannibal isle near the banks of the Nile,
    Where savages jump and roar;
With a big sharp knife may they take his life,
    While his vessel is still afloat,
And pick his bones as clean as stones,
    Is the prayer of poor Skin the Goat.

Anonymous

# Were Not the Gael Fallen

Were not the Gael fallen from their high estate
And Fola's warrior kings cast down by fate
And learning mocked in Eire's evil day,
I were no servant, Edmond, in thy pay.

Ye shall not stay my toil, once held divine,
Thou and thy fleering harlots at their wine,
Till all the brave are dead and out of reach
Eireamhon's people of the golden speech.

Edmond, I give good counsel. Heed it thou!
Leave mocking at my holy labours now,
Or such a rain of venomed shafts I'll send
That never a man shall save thee nor defend.

A tale I've heard that well might tame thy mood.
A gamesome chief of Gascony's best blood
Refused a poet once. The satire sped
And the man withered, strengthless, leprous, dead.

Peadar O'Mulconry
Translated by Robin Flower

# The Curse

*To a sister of an enemy of the author's
who disapproved of "The Playboy."*

Lord, confound this surly sister,
Blight her brow with blotch and blister,
Cramp her larynx, lung, and liver,
In her guts a galling give her.

Let her live to earn her dinners
In Mountjoy with seedy sinners:
Lord, this judgment quickly bring,
And I'm your servant, J. M. Synge.

John Millington Synge

# Ireland

From "silk o' the kine" to "the old sow that eats her farrow," Ireland has been known by many names and inspired conflicting emotions: a complexity not entirely to be captured in words.

# Let Erin Remember the Days of Old

Let Erin remember the days of old,
    Ere her faithless sons betray'd her;
When Malachi wore the collar of gold,
    Which he won from her proud invader,
When her kings, with standard of green unfurl'd,
    Led the Red-branch Knights to danger;—
Ere the emerald gem of the western world
    Was set in the crown of a stranger.

On Lough Neagh's bank, as the fisherman strays,
    When the clear cold eve's declining,
He sees the round towers of other days
    In the wave beneath him shining;
Thus shall memory often, in dreams sublime,
    Catch a glimpse of the days that are over;
Thus, sighing, look through the waves of time
    For the long faded glories they cover.

Thomas Moore

# Ireland

We Irish pride ourselves as patriots
and tell the beadroll of the valiant ones
since Clontarf's sunset saw the Norsemen broken...
Aye, and before that too we had our heroes:
but they were mighty fighters and victorious.
The later men got nothing save defeat,
hard transatlantic sidewalks or the scaffold...

We Irish, vainer than tense Lucifer,
are yet content with half-a-dozen turf,
and cry our adoration for a bog,
rejoicing in the rain that never ceases,
and happy to stride over the sterile acres,
or stony hills that scarcely feed a sheep.
But we are fools, I say, are ignorant fools
to waste the spirit's warmth in this cold air,
to spend our wit and love and poetry
on half-a-dozen peat and a black bog.

We are not native here or anywhere.
We were the keltic wave that broke over Europe,
and ran up this bleak beach among these stones:
but when the tide ebbed, were left stranded here

in crevices, and ledge-protected pools
that have grown salter with the drying up
of the great common flow that kept us sweet
with fresh cold draughts from deep down in the ocean.

So we are bitter, and are dying out
in terrible harshness in this lonely place,
and what we think is love for usual rock,
or old affection for our customary ledge,
is but forgotten longing for the sea
that cries far out and calls us to partake
in his great tidal movements round the earth.

John Hewitt

# Ireland

'Twas the dream of a God,
　And the mould of His hand,
That you shook 'neath His stroke,
That you trembled and broke,
　To this beautiful land.

Here He loosed from His hold
　A brown tumult of wings,
Till the wind on the sea
Bore the strange melody
　Of an island that sings.

He made you all fair,
　You in purple and gold,
You in silver and green,
Till no eye that has seen
　Without love can behold.

I have left you behind
　In the path of the past,
With the white breath of flowers,
With the best of God's hours,
　I have left you at last.

Dora Sigerson Shorter

# Memory of Brother Michael

It would never be morning, always evening,
Golden sunset, golden age—
When Shakespeare, Marlowe and Jonson were writing
The future of England page by page
A nettle-wild grave was Ireland's stage.

It would never be spring, always autumn
After a harvest always lost—
When Drake was winning seas for England
We sailed in puddles of the past
Pursuing the ghost of Brendan's mast.

The seeds among the dust were less than dust,
Dust we sought, decay,
The young sprout rising smothered in it
Cursed for being in the way—
And the same is true to-day.

Culture is always something that was,
Something pedants can measure:
Skull of bard, thigh of chief,
Depth of dried-up river.
Shall we be thus forever?
Shall we be thus forever?

Patrick Kavanagh

# Red Hanrahan's Song about Ireland

The old brown thorn trees break in two high over
    Cummen Strand,
Under a bitter black wind that blows from the left hand;
Our courage breaks like an old tree in a black wind and dies,
But we have hidden in our hearts the flame out of the eyes
Of Cathleen, the daughter of Houlihan.*

The wind has bundled up the clouds high over Knocknarea,
And thrown the thunder on the stones for all that Maeve
    can say.
Angers that are like noisy clouds have set our hearts abeat;
But we have all bent low and low and kissed the quiet feet
Of Cathleen, the daughter of Houlihan.

The yellow pool has overflowed high up on Clooth-na-Bare,
For the wet winds are blowing out of the clinging air;
Like heavy flooded waters our bodies and our blood;
But purer than a tall candle before the Holy Rood
Is Cathleen, the daughter of Houlihan.

**William Butler Yeats**

*Cathleen Ní Houlihan is an ancient personification of Ireland.

# Ireland

That ragged
leaking raft held
between sea and sea

its long
forgotten cable melting
into deeper darkness where,

at the root
of it, the slow
sea circles and chews.

Nightly the dark-
ness lands like hands
to mine downwards, springing

tiny leaks
till dawn finds
field is bog, bog lake.

Richard Ryan

# Windharp

*for Patrick Collins*

The sounds of Ireland,
that restless whispering
you never get away
from, seeping out of
low bushes and grass,
heatherbells and fern,
wrinkling bog pools,
scraping tree branches,
light hunting cloud,
sound hounding sight,
a hand ceaselessly
combing and stroking
the landscape, till
the valley gleams
like the pile upon
a mountain pony's coat.

John Montague

# Index

# Acknowledgments

THE EDITOR GRATEFULLY acknowledges the permission of writers and publishers to reprint the following copyright material:

Austin Clarke
"Mable Kelly" from *Flight to Africa*, reprinted by permission of R. Dardis Clarke, 21 Pleasant Street, Dublin 8, Ireland.

Robin Flower
"Were Not the Gael" and "The Flight of the Earls" from *The Irish Tradition* (1947), reprinted by permission of Oxford University Press.

Seamus Heaney
"Requiem for the Croppies," "Traditions" from *Poems 1965-1975* by Seamus Heaney. Copyright © 1980 by Seamus Heaney, reprinted by permission of Farrar, Straus & Giroux, Inc.

John Hewitt
"Ireland," reprinted by permission of The Blackstaff Press.

Patrick Kavanagh
"Shandocuff" and "Memory of Brother Michael" copyright Devin-Adair, Publishers, Inc., Old Greenwich, CT 06870, reprinted by permission of the publisher. All rights reserved.

Medbh McGuckian
"The Dream Language of Fergus" from *On Ballycastle Beach*, reprinted by permission of Wake Forest University Press.

John Montague
"A Grafted Tongue" and "The Flight of the Earls" from *The Rough Field* in *John Montague: Collected Poems.* "Windharp" from *A Slow Dance* in *John Montague: Collected Poems.* All reprinted by permission of Wake Forest University Press.

Paul Muldoon
"Armageddon, Armageddon" part II from *Mules and Early Poems,* reprinted by permission of Wake Forest University Press.

Nuala Ní Dhomhnaill
"Nude," translated by Paul Muldoon, from *Pharaoh's Daughter*, reprinted by permission of Wake Forest University Press. "Labasheedy" from *Selected Poems*, reprinted by permission of the author.

Richard Ryan
"Ireland" from *Ravenswood* (Dublin: Dolmen Press, 1973), reprinted by permission of Colin Smythe Ltd on behalf of the author.

James Simmons
"The Influence of Natural Objects" from *Poems 1956-1986* (1986), reprinted by kind permission of the author and The Gallery Press.

William Butler Yeats
"Sailing to Byzantium" from *The Poems of W.B Yeats: A New Edition*, edited by Richard J. Finneran, reprinted by permission of Simon & Schuster. Copyright 1928 by Macmillan Publishing Company, copyright renewed © 1956 by Georgie Yeats.

While every care has been taken to clear permission for the use of copyrighted material, in case of accidental infringement, copyright holders are asked to write to the editor care of the publishers.